Praise for *Heart of a Competitor*

"Athletics can be a great way to learn lessons about everyday life. But what is really special is when you can take athletic lessons and apply them to your spiritual life. *Heart of a Competitor* takes a look at how the tests we face as players and coaches can help us grow as Christians."

Tony Dungy
former head coach, Indianapolis Colts

"In the *Heart of a Competitor*, you will see that it is just as important to train spiritually as it is to train physically and mentally. When you focus on training the total body, it will take you to the next level."

Tamika Catchings
WNBA player, the Indiana Fever;
founder, Catch the Stars Foundation;
four-time Olympic Gold Medalist

"*Heart of a Competitor* is an awesome resource for believers—both on and off the field. Life isn't always about winning a game; it's about living for the Lord in all that we do. This book helps to keep that in perspective."

Clayton Kershaw
Major League Baseball pitcher;
author, *Arise*; National League
Cy Young Award Winner (2011)

HEART

OF A

COMPETITOR

PLAYBOOK

FELLOWSHIP OF CHRISTIAN ATHLETES

HEART
OF A
COMPETITOR
▶PLAYBOOK◀

DAILY DEVOTIONS
FOR A WINNING ATTITUDE

Revell

a division of Baker Publishing Group
Grand Rapids, Michigan

Published by Revell
a division of Baker Publishing Group
P.O. Box 6287, Grand Rapids, MI 49516–6287
www.revellbooks.com

Some material adapted from *Heart of a Competitor*, published in 2013 by Regal Books

ISBN 978-0-8007-2810-6

Printed in the United States of America

Unless otherwise indicated, Scripture quotations are from the Holman Christian Standard Bible®, copyright © 1999, 2000, 2002, 2003, 2009 by Holman Bible Publishers. Used by permission. Holman Christian Standard Bible®, Holman CSB®, and HCSB® are federally registered trademarks of Holman Bible Publishers.

Scripture quotations labeled ESV are from The Holy Bible, English Standard Version® (ESV®), copyright © 2001 by Crossway, a publishing ministry of Good News Publishers. Used by permission. All rights reserved. ESV Text Edition: 2011

Scripture quotations labeled NLT are from the *Holy Bible*, New Living Translation, copyright © 1996, 2004, 2015 by Tyndale House Foundation. Used by permission of Tyndale House Publishers, Inc., Carol Stream, Illinois 60188. All rights reserved.

17 18 19 20 21 22 23   7 6 5 4 3 2 1

Contents

Letter from FCA

Dear Teammate,

The mark of a true competitor is found in the heart. Here is where every competitive passion begins and where our relationship with God is grown. These thirty-one devotionals are written from a competitor's mind-set and include Bible verses to help you understand God's perspective on key issues. It doesn't matter if you are a coach or an athlete, if you play on a team or compete on an individual level, these devotions will teach you how to live out your faith as a competitor.

Our hope is that this book will motivate you, over the course of one month, to develop a consistent, focused way of spending time with God, so you will deepen your understanding of His Word and become a true competitor for

Jesus Christ. We call these intentional times of reading God's Word "Training Times." You can read more about developing a consistent Training Time in the Introduction.

As a competitor, you have been given a tremendous platform from which to influence others. We pray that God will use these devotions to transform your life as a competitor so that you can make an eternal impact for Jesus Christ.

Make an Impact,
The Fellowship of Christian Athletes

Introduction

Training Time

In sports, time-outs give athletes and coaches a chance to strategize for upcoming challenges. Similarly, in life, we need to take time-outs to think about our purpose as members of God's team. FCA is excited to present you with a collection of devotions that will challenge you to play and live for the glory of God. Each devotion is written from an athletic perspective and will encourage you to be more like Christ both on and off the field.

Every day, set aside a special quiet time to be with God. During this spiritual training time, talk to God and let Him speak to you through the Bible. There are many effective methods that can be used for your daily time with God. One method that we recommend is the PRESS method.

The PRESS Method

Pray

Begin your quiet time by thanking God for the new day, and then ask Him to help you learn from what you're about to read. Prepare yourself by

- clearing your mind and being quiet before the Lord
- asking God to settle your heart
- listening to worship music to prepare your spirit
- asking God to give you a teachable heart

Read

Begin with the thirty-one devotionals provided in this book. Also, try reading a chapter of Proverbs every day (there are thirty-one chapters in the book of Proverbs, which makes it ideal for daily reading), one psalm, and/or a chapter out of the Old or New Testament. You may consider beginning with one of the Gospels (Matthew, Mark, Luke, or John), or one of the shorter letters, such as Ephesians or James.

Examine

Ask yourself the following questions with regard to the passage you read:

- *Teaching:* What do I need to *know* about God, myself, and others?
- *Rebuking:* What do I need to *stop* doing—sins, habits, or selfish patterns?
- *Correcting:* What do I need to *change* in my thoughts, attitudes, or actions?
- *Training:* What do I need to *do* in obedience to God's leading?

Summarize

Do one of the following:

- Discover what the passage reveals about God and His character, what it says or promises about you, and what it says or promises about others (such as your parents, friends, or teammates). Write your thoughts down in a personal journal.
- Rewrite one or two key verses in your own words.
- Outline what each verse is saying.
- Give each verse a one-word title that summarizes what it says.

Share

Talk with God about what you've learned. Also, take time each day to share with another person what you learned during that day's study. Having a daily training time is the key to spiritual development. If you commit to working through these thirty-one devotionals over the next month, you will establish this as a habit—one that will be vital to your growth in Christ.

If you are committed to establishing this daily training time with God, fill out the box below.

I will commit to establishing a daily habit of spending time with God.

Signed _____

Today's Date _____

Writers

We have invited athletes, coaches, and team chaplains from all levels (in addition to FCA staff) to contribute their time, talent, and experience in writing these devotions. These writers come from diverse backgrounds and include representatives from a variety of sports, including baseball, soccer, basketball, football, lacrosse, track and field, and others.

Format

Ready A verse or passage of Scripture that focuses or directs your heart and mind. Turn to the Scripture reference in your Bible and read it within the overall context of the passage.

Set A teaching point (a story, training point, or thought taken from a sports perspective) that draws a lesson from the passage.

Go Questions that will help you examine your heart and challenge you to apply God's truth to your life—on and off the field.

Workout Additional Scripture references to help you dig deeper.

Overtime A closing prayer that will help you commit to the Lord what you have learned.

To receive the daily email devotional "FCA's Impact Play," go to www.FCA.org.

1

Trust God

MIKE FISHER

Ready

> "Trust in the LORD with all your heart; do not depend on your own understanding. Seek his will in all you do, and he will show you which path to take."—Proverbs 3:5–6 (NLT)

Set

As a young athlete, I did my best to balance my hockey career with my faith. At the age of nineteen, my faith was tested when I suffered a serious knee injury. After the game, I knew I was done for the year. My mom called me and said, "Remember, God doesn't make mistakes. Trust in Him and it will be okay. He'll use it for good." At the time, I didn't want to hear it, but in the long run, she was right.

You can hope that everything is going to be perfect, but God doesn't promise that life will be free of troubles. We won't always understand why we're struggling or why things aren't going our way. But He does promise that if we put our trust completely in Him, He will take care of our needs and give us the strength to make it through the trials of life.

Trust takes time. We all love to be in control. I can tell you from experience that it's freeing when you begin to give that up. Ultimately, the most important decision you can make is to give your life over to Christ and trust Him with it. When you can do that, your fears will begin to fade and your trust in Him will begin to grow.

Go

1. What are some areas where you find it easy to trust God? With what areas of your life do you find it difficult to trust God?

2. How does fear impact your ability to trust God? How can you overcome this fear?

3. What are some things with which you need to do a better job trusting God?

Workout

Matthew 6:25–34; Romans 8:28–31; Psalm 37:4–6; Joshua 1:9

Overtime

Lord, help me to surrender my thirst for control and trust You more in every area of my life, including sports. Relieve me of my fear and doubt and allow me to see Your power moving in my life. Amen.

journal

journal

2

Game Face

SEAN MCNAMARA

Ready

> "The Lord GOD will help Me; therefore I have not been humiliated; therefore I have set My face like flint, and I know I will not be put to shame."—Isaiah 50:7

Set

The lacrosse game was heading in the wrong direction fast. As a goalie, I was frustrated that our defense had allowed three quick goals in a short period of time. Our coach pulled me aside and said, "Wipe that look off your face! If your teammates see or think that you, as our leader, doubt for one second that we can win this game, they will be discouraged and give up." It was obvious that I had lost my "game face."

Although circumstances, like my lacrosse game, continually change, we need to resolve, like Isaiah, to make our faces like flint or stone. Today, we wouldn't say "get your flint face on" but rather "get your game face on." As competitors, we know what it means to have a game face. However, do we know what it means to put on our game face when it comes to our spiritual lives?

As followers of Christ, our spiritual game face doesn't come from our own resolve, perseverance, or tenacity. Instead, our game face comes from putting our trust in God, knowing that Christ has gained victory over our sin at the resurrection (1 Cor. 15:57). We don't know what tomorrow may bring, but as Christians, our countenance and demeanor should be unwavering, because we trust the promises of God's Word. Coaches and athletes, we are confident because our confidence lies in Christ, not in this world.

Go

1. Why is it so hard for us as competitors to place our confidence in Christ?

2. Name a person in the Bible, on your team, or in your life who is flint-faced and determined in trusting God. What can you learn from them?

3. What can you do today to move your confidence from yourself to Christ? Name three different ways to accomplish this.

Workout

Romans 5:35; Revelation 12:11; 1 Corinthians 15:50–57

Overtime

Lord, thank You that my hope in You transcends all circumstances. I desire to put on a spiritual game face every day and in every circumstance. I place my trust and confidence in Your character and in the promises of Your Word. Amen.

journal

journal

3

Never Give Up

JAYSON GEE

Ready

"Dear brothers and sisters, when troubles of any kind come your way, consider it an opportunity for great joy. For you know that when your faith is tested, your endurance has a chance to grow. So let it grow, for when your endurance is fully developed, you will be perfect and complete, needing nothing."—James 1:2–4 (NLT)

Set

When I was an overweight junior varsity player who mostly sat on the bench keeping stats for the rest of the team, I wanted to quit basketball altogether. But my mom encouraged me to stick it out. "You're going to start for the varsity team next year!" she boldly declared.

It didn't make sense at the time, but my mom had the foresight to see the potential in me that I couldn't see for myself. Along with the help of two influential coaches in my life, I dropped nearly thirty pounds, became one of the varsity's top players, and earned a scholarship to play at the University of Charleston.

Several years later, I faced an even greater challenge when my ten-year-old son Brandon was diagnosed with paranoid schizophrenia. Brandon's outward behaviors were obvious. The doctors showed me the results of the tests to back up their claim that he would be institutionalized for the rest of his life. But God had revealed to me that Brandon was going to be healed one day. So I made the decision to act on that promise and persevere through the difficult days that followed.

If you've never faced any major troubles in your life, you will someday. That's just life. When bad situations come, stay the course. Keep believing in God. Trust His voice over everyone else's. With

His help, you will have the endurance to persevere through any challenges you might face.

Go

1. Describe a difficult time that tested your faith. How did you respond to the test?
2. How is it possible to experience joy in the midst of a trial? Can you name a time when you experienced this?
3. What are some specific ways that God can strengthen your endurance and increase your faith? Name three.

Workout

James 1:12; Colossians 1:11–12; Romans 5:3–5; Hebrews 12:1–15

Overtime

Lord, thank You for Your grace and mercy. Build up my endurance through prayer and devotion so I can be ready for the difficult times in my life. Amen.

journal

journal

4

Overcome Adversity

Tamika Catchings

Ready

> "No, in all these things we are more than victorious through Him who loved us."—Romans 8:37

Set

As a child, I dealt with the embarrassment of having to wear glasses and braces. And to make matters worse, I had problems with my hearing, which required me to wear a hearing aid and affected my speech. You can imagine the name-calling that ensued. I remember one day on the way home from school, I was so frustrated that I took off my hearing aid and threw it into a ditch. Needless to say, my parents weren't too happy about that.

By the time I was in middle school, my parents divorced and added another layer of adversity to my life. I used sports as an escape from my problems. But even there, I faced my share of difficulties. Throughout my career I've torn my ACL, my meniscus, and my Achilles tendon. When I faced those tough times, it would have been easy to give up and say, "Woe is me!" But I represent God in everything I do, and I knew He had a plan for my life. And through those injuries and struggles, I drew closer to the Lord.

God has a plan for everyone and once you've discovered that plan, no one but you can stop it from coming to pass. This has certainly been true in my life. I have personally experienced what it means to be "victorious through Him who loved us." And all of the things I've experienced have given me a platform to inspire others and share with them the love of God. By His grace, those adversities made me stronger and helped me become the person that I am today.

Go

1. What are some adversities that you have faced within and outside of sports? How did you handle these situations?
2. Read Romans 8:28. Are you able to see how God has used difficult situations in your life for the greater good? Explain.
3. Do you truly believe that God has a plan for your life? How might embracing His plan help you deal with life's challenges?

Workout

Romans 8:28; 2 Corinthians 4:8–9; Philippians 4:12–13; 2 Corinthians 12:9–10

Overtime

Lord, I know that I am victorious through You, who loves me. Help me to see Your purpose for my life. Give me the strength to overcome adversity that seeks to discourage me from fulfilling Your ultimate plan. In Your mighty name. Amen.

journal

journal

5

Vision Eyes

Dan Britton

Ready

"Indeed, the Lord GOD does nothing without revealing His counsel to His servants the prophets."
—Amos 3:7

Set

At age two, Craig MacFarlane was blinded in a tragic accident, but he turned his defeat into victory by becoming a world-class athlete who won over one hundred gold medals in sports like wrestling, track and field, and downhill skiing. He has even shot a 91 in golf! Craig doesn't have his eyesight, but he does have a powerful inner vision that fuels his drive to overcome. As a result, he has motivated millions with his vision!

It has been said, "One person with vision in their eyes can multiply and change the world!" Since the beginning of sports, athletes and coaches who have inner vision have shaped and changed history. There was a vision that was birthed deep in their souls and it changed the way they lived—and the way others lived too. They had vision eyes.

Every vision needs to have three key ingredients. To determine if you have a God vision, not just a good vision, answer these three questions:

1. Is your vision too small?

   If your vision doesn't terrify you, then it is too small. A God vision should be so huge that you are bound to fail unless God steps in. You must get the "no way!" response when you share your vision. How big is your vision? The first ingredient of a God vision is terror.

2. Is your vision too narrow?

   If your vision doesn't include others, then it is too narrow. Having a vision doesn't mean you against the world. A God vision has to include others. God will rise up a multitude to embrace and own your vision. The second ingredient of a God vision is others.

3. Is your vision just a daydream?

   If your vision doesn't get accomplished, then it is just a daydream. Too many people talk about what they are going to do and never produce any results. A God vision always gets done. It's not just talk. Take one step toward accomplishing the vision that God has birthed in your heart. The third ingredient of a God vision is accomplishment.

Don't let the pace of life, negative thinking, or even doubts and fears kill your vision. Athletes and coaches, do whatever it takes to hear from God over the noise of life and pursue the vision He's planted in your soul. One person with inner vision can multiply and change the world!

Go

1. Does your vision terrify you? Why?
2. How can you incorporate more people into your vision?
3. Have you been able to start what you have been longing to do? Make a plan to make your vision a reality.

Workout

Proverbs 29:18; Habakkuk 2:3

Overtime

Father, give me a vision so big that I am bound to fail unless You step in. I don't want to get stuck in the trap of a dream that is too small, too narrow, or just a daydream. Help me to ignore the noise of life and pursue the vision You have given me. Use me to impact the world. Amen.

journal

journal

6

Love God, Love Others

ELANA MEYERS-TAYLOR

Ready

"Jesus replied, '"You must love the Lord your God with all your heart, all your soul, and all your mind." This is the first and greatest commandment. A second is equally important: "Love your neighbor as yourself."'"—Matthew 22:37–39 (NLT)

Set

When I was nine years old, I decided I wanted to be an Olympian. I tried softball, basketball, soccer, track, and any other sport that might help me fulfill that dream. Then, in a strange turn of events, I earned a spot on the USA Women's National Bobsled Team and won two Olympic medals and three World Championships.

Being an Olympian is one of the greatest honors I can ever imagine. But I've learned that my purpose is much higher than representing my country as an elite athlete. I've learned that I am on this planet to serve God, and I can do that only if I love Him and love others.

For me, that means loving everyone within my sport—even the athletes against whom I compete. Sometimes, that love is expressed through a giving attitude. If one of my fellow competitors needs equipment or help with a problem, I'm going to do what I can for them, regardless of what team they are on. It's not easy. It's hard to show that kind of love for others, but that's what I'm called by God to do.

There's nothing like winning an Olympic medal or a World Championship. But there's nothing better than the peace and contentment that comes from obeying God's two greatest commands. Loving God and loving others will fulfill you like no other achievement, award, or material thing you might be chasing.

Go

1. What do you think it means to love God "with all your heart, all your soul, and all your mind"? How can you do this on a daily basis with your team, family, and community?

2. What are some things that keep you from loving others as you love yourself? How can you overcome these things?

3. How can you be more intentional in showing love (as a family member, as a student, as a friend, and as an athlete)? Name three different ways.

Workout

John 13:34; 1 John 4:7–21; Matthew 5:43–48; 1 Corinthians 13:1–7

Overtime

Lord, help me to love You more every day and to be more intentional in showing love to others. Fill me with Your love until it spills over and touches everyone who crosses my path. I want to complete the purpose for which I was created. Amen.

journal

7

Giving Your All

BLAKE ELDER

Ready

"Summoning His disciples, He said to them, 'I assure you: This poor widow has put in more than all those giving to the temple treasury. For they all gave out of their surplus, but she out of her poverty has put in everything she possessed—all she had to live on.'"—Mark 12:43–44

Set

There are many things that I count as a privilege in my athletic career. Playing football for Appalachian

State, beating then-ranked No. 5 University of Michigan, and winning two Division I FCS national championships are at the top of the list. But the greatest privilege I've had was the opportunity to play for Coach Jerry Moore. He is a man of faith, integrity, and passion. He had a slogan that we lived by: "What are you willing to give up?" His giving character fueled me and my teammates to be men who gave our all for what we believed in, and it showed on and off the field.

Jesus is attracted to those who give their all, like the poor widow mentioned in Mark 12. She gave all that she had monetarily. She laid her entire livelihood down, believing that it would make a difference. It wasn't the amount as it compared to others or her circumstances that determined what she would give. Out of a selfless commitment to something larger than herself she gave everything that she had, knowing she was being faithful to her calling.

When circumstances get tough and the odds are against you, what you are willing to give will make a difference in your life. It shows the level of your commitment to a cause greater than yourself, inspiring others to do the same. So, what are you willing to give for your sport—or better yet, your Savior?

Go

1. Do your teammates recognize you as a giver or a taker? Why do you think they see you this way?
2. Do you tend to let negative circumstances and momentum determine whether you give your all? How can you overcome this?
3. How can you prepare yourself to not withhold what you should give, both physically and spiritually? Name three different ways.

Workout

Proverbs 11:24–25; 2 Corinthians 9:6–11; Mark 6:33–44

Overtime

Lord, thank You for giving Your best to me in Your Son, Jesus. I see that I am to be a giver, both on and off the field. I pray, in the name of Jesus, that You would give me the strength to give all that I have to represent You in all circumstances. Amen.

journal

journal

8

Identity Theft

KERRY O'NEILL

Ready

"Set your minds on what is above, not on what is on the earth. For you have died, and your life is hidden with the Messiah in God."—Colossians 3:2–3

Set

Each year millions of people become victims of identity theft. It is a crime that leaves the victim feeling violated and their life totally disrupted.

Another epidemic is the loss of identity in Christ. One might argue that it is also considered identity theft; that the enemy who comes to steal, kill, and destroy—the one who is the accuser of the brethren—is guilty of identity theft in the lives of countless Christians.

Think of your thoughts, words, and actions from the time before you had a relationship with Christ. Perhaps your identity as a competitor was marked by anger, comparison, or a performance-based value system. Now, your identity is in Christ. He loves you regardless of your performance in sports or life. There is nothing great you could do to make Him love you more; there is nothing awful you could do to make Him love you less. He loves you that much! Yet, the enemy will try to steal your identity in Christ, and the old habits of basing your worth on your performance can sneak back into your life.

However, the loss of identity in Christ is more preventable than financial identity theft. The key is reminding yourself who you truly are: who you are according to God, as He has described in His Word. You are a saint, a new creation, Christ's friend, and a light to the world. Start reminding Satan of these truths each time he tempts you with thoughts of the past or false beliefs about yourself and your relationship with Christ. Know who you are in Christ and don't back down.

Go

1. What does the Bible say regarding your new identity in Christ?
2. In what ways has the enemy tried to steal your identity in Christ? How can you prevent this from happening in the future?
3. Think of one Bible verse on which you can meditate to remember who you are in Christ. Memorize this verse and post it in a place that you will see on a daily basis.

Workout

John 1:12; Colossians 1:13; 1 Thessalonians 5:5

Overtime

Lord, help me remember who I am in You—a new creation and a light to the world. Give me strength to fight off the temptation to think any less of myself than what is revealed in Your Word. Amen.

journal

journal

9

Shine Your Light

TOBIN HEATH

Ready

"In the same way, let your light shine before others, so that they may see your good works and give glory to your Father who is in heaven."—Matthew 5:16 (ESV)

Set

I was just twenty years old when I first joined the United States Women's National Soccer Team. As the youngest member, it was hard to imagine that I had influence over others. But it didn't take me long to realize how big my platform truly was.

While some athletes cringe at the idea of being a role model, I am thankful for the opportunity to share the love of Jesus with others. Becoming known in my sport isn't what drives me to work hard. It's Jesus. That's why I play. I play to glorify Him.

My soccer career isn't about worldly outcomes in terms of winning or losing. It's about Jesus being known—not in a way that forces it on other people, but in a way that lets people know how He has transformed my life and given me purpose, meaning, love, and satisfaction. That's the message of Jesus. It's not a platform to impose on people. It's a platform to love people.

I worship God with the gifts He has given me. That's my motivation when I step out on the field every day. I'm just a vessel to share those gifts with others and hopefully allow His love to shine through everything I do.

Go

1. How would you describe your platform as an athlete? Are you using this platform to point others to Jesus Christ?

2. What do you think it means to "let your light shine before others"?

3. What are some ways that you can begin to set an example for others within your circle of influence on your team, in your family, and within your community?

Workout

1 Corinthians 11:1; 2 Corinthians 5:20; Philippians 2:12–15; 1 Thessalonians 1:6

Overtime

Lord, give me the courage and boldness to use my platform in a way that glorifies You and shows people Your love. I want to use my gifts as a light in the darkness. I want people to see You in everything I do. Amen.

journal

journal

10

Influence
with Integrity

ADAM WAINWRIGHT

Ready

"The one who lives with integrity lives securely,
but whoever perverts his ways will be found out."
—Proverbs 10:9

Set

In today's world of sports, it seems that anything
done for an advantage is fair game—as long as you
don't get caught. As a major league pitcher, I've seen

it all. Managers who spend their entire careers stealing the signs of other coaches from the dugouts and down the baselines. Players who reach base doing the same thing. Pitchers who are supposed to throw a clean, unscratched ball but discover that you can do some pretty cool things with a scuffed baseball.

As Christians, however, we are held to a higher standard. Our goal should be to live a life that's pleasing to God and that allows us to have influence on those around us. People seem to gravitate toward those who do things the right way. If you're not living with integrity, your influence will quickly be torn down. If you're not trusted, then your relationships will have little eternal significance.

In the book of Daniel, we read about a young man who lived with great integrity. When given the chance to turn his back on God's commands, Daniel stood strong and gained influence over an entire kingdom. And of course, there has been no greater example of integrity than Jesus Christ. He was who He said He was and lived a sinless life despite many opportunities to succumb to temptation.

Living with integrity in this day and age isn't easy. You might say it's harder than ever before. But with God's Word and the Holy Spirit guiding your steps, it is possible to be the person of integrity that He created you to be.

Go

1. What are some things that make it difficult to maintain integrity in today's world? Why is it difficult to maintain integrity for you personally?
2. How would you define the relationship between integrity and influence?
3. What can you start doing today that will help set you on a path toward godly integrity? Name three different things.

Workout

Daniel 1; Proverbs 28:6; Psalm 41:11–12

Overtime

Lord, I want to walk upright in Your sight. Give me the determination to live with integrity in all that I say and do. Help me build trust within my relationships so that I might influence others for Your kingdom. Amen.

journal

journal

11

Linger Longer

DAN BRITTON

Ready

"Where can I go to escape Your Spirit? Where can I flee from Your presence?"—Psalm 139:7

Set

Unfortunately, as athletes and coaches we often approach our daily devotional time as something that needs to get done due to our "conquer it" attitude. Something like this: *"I rise. I read. I am done!"* Now we can get on with the day. It becomes an action item that gets checked off the to-do list, because we love the feeling of accomplishment. Our mind-set toward devotions is like taking medicine or eating spinach; something that we *have to do* instead of *long to do*.

A daily devotion becomes all about us—what we can get out of it and how much we need it. Yes, we do desperately need it, but we also need to realize that God longs for us to be with Him. The Lord delights when we sit at His feet each day and linger in His presence. Stopping the chaos of the day by stepping away from all the clutter and being consumed by His love is a nonnegotiable.

Too many people go through the motions. No spiritual grit. No investment made for the long term. When we think survival, our devotional time becomes a matter of just getting us through the day. We're not thinking of what's down the road. We're running on spiritual fumes instead of having a full tank. Soaking in God's presence daily moves us from spiritually surviving to spiritually thriving.

Lingering longer allows us to hear God's voice. There will always be an opportunity to pour out what the Lord has poured in. He will always use our extra soaking for His work. But we need to stop the rushing, drop to our knees or fall on our face, and soak in His glorious presence. Sit at the feet of Jesus and wait for Him to speak. We need to listen to the Holy Spirit instead of filling the time with our words. Linger in His presence and find out what's on God's heart.

We need to STOP–DROP–SOAK. STOP daily, DROP before the Lord, and SOAK in His presence. Stopping is our discipline; dropping is our posture; and soaking is our worship. Extend your time with the Savior and enjoy His presence!

Go

1. Have you soaked in God's presence before? Have you made some extended time to stop, drop, and soak? Write down a plan for the next week to soak in His presence.
2. What about your quiet time can you change in order to listen better?
3. How can soaking in God's presence help the stress you face as a competitor?

Workout

Psalms 27:14; 62:5

Overtime

Lord, help me to linger longer in Your presence today. Too often I go through the motions in my spiritual life, and I find myself running on fumes. Open my ears and heart to hear from Your Spirit. I want to stop, drop, and soak every day. Amen.

journal

journal

12

Stay Accountable

CLINT HURDLE

Ready

> "Confess your sins to each other and pray for
> each other so that you may be healed. The earnest
> prayer of a righteous person has great power and
> produces wonderful results."—James 5:16 (NLT)

Set

I've been involved in the game of baseball most
of my life, and one thing I can tell you for certain:
there's no way individual players can be successful

over a long period of time when they try to do things on their own. I didn't understand the spiritual nature of that truth until much later in life.

I went to church as a young boy and accepted Christ while in high school. But back then my personal relationship with Jesus was like an ATM card. I communicated with Him only when I needed something. There was really no accountability for following God's Word or serving Him.

When I turned forty, I realized I needed to plug back into my relationship with Christ. It was during that part of my journey when I realized that isolation is one of the most dangerous situations in which we can find ourselves. I needed to surround myself with some strong Christian men who would keep me accountable to my commitment. For me, that meant becoming more active in my local church and attending Bible study groups. It also meant getting involved in FCA and baseball chapel.

We need to stay plugged in to something, and that starts with prayer and the reading of God's Word. But we also need other believers to keep us accountable, to challenge us, and to encourage us to stay the course.

Go

1. Can you describe a time when you tried to perform a difficult task on your own? How did that situation turn out? In retrospect, how might you change the way you performed that difficult task?

2. Do you find it easy or difficult to ask others for help with spiritual matters? Explain.

3. What are some things you can do today that will help you stay more accountable to your commitment to God in the future? Name three different things.

Workout

Ecclesiastes 4:9–12; Proverbs 19:20–21; 27:17; Hebrews 10:24–25

Overtime

Lord, surround me with other believers who can build me up spiritually and challenge and encourage me as I walk this journey with You. I want to stay accountable to my commitment and honor You in everything I do. Amen.

journal

journal

13

Coming Back after Injury

ROGER LIPE

Ready

"Therefore, since Christ suffered in the flesh, equip yourselves also with the same resolve—because the one who suffered in the flesh has finished with sin."—1 Peter 4:1

Set

Who has more confidence about recovering from injury—the one who has never been hurt, or the player who has come through the pain and has found renewed strength? If the answer seems obvious, you may have never been injured.

The apostle Peter makes mention of suffering and its results in the above Scripture verse. He's not saying that after we've suffered we're somehow exempt from making moral mistakes, rather that suffering changes our mind-set and leads us to live for more than physical gratification.

Before we've suffered any significant injury, many of us play a little tentatively in dangerous situations. There is a latent fear that if we risk a possible injury, we can never recover or play the same again. However, in the player who has suffered and recovered, that indecision and fear is overcome by the assurance that even if this daring play leads to pain, he or she can come through it to compete even more strongly.

As you compete today, play with strength, courage, and tenacity. Don't be intimidated by the potential injury that you imagine could wreck your playing career. And to those of you who have come through injury, who have suffered in the flesh, loan some courage to your teammates and play with great passion.

Go

1. How have the injuries that you have suffered led you to a greater confidence and a more passionate approach to competition?
2. What do you think it means to share in Christ's sufferings? Have you experienced this before?
3. How does experiencing such sufferings help you overcome temptation, habitual sins, and other trials?

Workout

1 Corinthians 10:13; James 1:12; 1 Peter 1:6

Overtime

Lord, I pray for the strength to bear the burden of Your cross with courage and assurance, knowing You are always with me. Help me to use my experiences to encourage other believers to do the same. Amen.

journal

journal

14

Gold with God

REX STUMP

Ready

"For all have sinned and fall short of the glory of God. They are justified freely by His grace through the redemption that is in Christ Jesus."—Romans 3:23–24

Set

The 2012 Summer Olympics were full of excitement and surprises. There were moments of exhilaration as athletes excelled and won in an unexpected manner, and then there were moments of disappointment when the favored team failed to win gold. In spite of our predictions or expectations, results can never fully be calculated ahead of time.

Olympic gymnast Gabby Douglas was expected to win on the uneven bars. When she fell short of her goal, many avid followers were perplexed. The 2011 world vaulting champion, gymnast McKayla Maroney, was poised to walk away with Olympic gold but ended up with silver. Instead of celebrating, many Americans were stunned with disappointment.

Spiritually speaking, many of us believe that our actions are good enough to win gold with God. But as the apostle Paul says in Romans, we all have sinned and fallen short of perfection. We make mistakes. There are deductions and flaws in our lives, proving it impossible to win gold with God.

But through His love and grace, God has made a way to be right with Him. He sent His Son Jesus Christ to this earth to live a perfect, gold-medal life and become the ultimate sacrifice for us! And Romans 3:22 tells us that by placing our faith in Jesus Christ, our mistakes are wiped out and we "win gold" with God. It's that easy. Through His forgiveness and help, we can live a spiritually golden life!

Go

1. Have you ever expected a win, only to face defeat? How did you react to the situation?
2. Are you trying to live a perfect life without God? How so?
3. Have you received God's love and grace to forgive your sins? If not, take time to do so today.

Workout

Romans 3; Luke 7:36–50

Overtime

Heavenly Father, I have fallen short and made mistakes. Thank You for loving me and making a way for me to be right in Your eyes. Please forgive me. Pick me up and help me live a victorious life for You! Amen.

journal

journal

15

Do the Right Thing

HAL HIATT

Ready

> "The one who lives with integrity will be helped,
> but one who distorts right and wrong will sud-
> denly fall."—Proverbs 28:18

Set

There are eight seconds left in the game, and we are
down by two points. The buzzer has just sounded
from our last time-out, and we have the final play
ready. We throw the ball in, and everyone is hustling

to their place on the court. The play is working as planned, and our best shooter receives the ball for a wide-open three pointer. And then it happens.

Out of nowhere the other team's big man steps out of the paint and jumps high to deflect the shot. As he does, instead of the ball traveling toward the basket, it is swatted right into my hands and I'm wide open. There is just enough time to pull the trigger for a final shot, and I toss the ball at the basket. Just as the buzzer sounds, my desperation shot clears the bottom of the net. The referee signals that the basket is a three-pointer, and we win the game!

But there is a problem. I look down and realize that my left foot was clearly out of bounds when I took the shot. There was no referee close to me and evidently I'm the only one who noticed. My whole team is celebrating what looks like a *big* win. I realize that telling the truth in this situation could cost my team a trip to the conference championship game. What should I do?

Go

1. The Bible verse today says that the "blameless will be rescued." What does that mean to you?

2. Is it harder to tell the truth when it is costly to others? Why or why not?

3. How do you overcome the temptation of not being honest when you know it will be costly to others and yourself?

Workout

Psalms 15; 51:6; Acts 24:16; Luke 16:10

Overtime

Father, help me in all of my decisions to live with integrity and do the right thing, even when it is costly to others and myself. Amen.

journal

journal

16

What's at Your Center?

Joe Matera

Ready

"Jesus said to her, 'I am the resurrection and the life. The one who believes in Me, even if he dies, will live. Everyone who lives and believes in Me will never die—ever. Do you believe this?'"
—John 11:25–26

Set

As athletes and coaches, we are motivated to think, "I can handle anything that comes my way!" We are trained to take on tough opponents and push ourselves beyond our limits. I am used to having challenges, but on my fifty-second birthday I was faced with news that I couldn't handle. I was diagnosed with stage IV cancer and given six months to live. I was a surfer with an active lifestyle and no obvious health issues. The C word was the furthest thing from my mind, and the news was like a huge tsunami washing over my family.

In the days that followed, my family and I discovered that my diagnosis was taking its toll on all of us. The problem was that our focus was now cancer. Imagine the nucleus of an atom; cancer was now the center of our family, and we were revolving around an unknown entity that was trying to destroy us. We decided right then to pray and ask the Lord to be our center, that He and our family together would be the nucleus. With God's power we pushed cancer to the outer rim of the atom, making it seem smaller, having less influence on our lives. It was just something that we were dealing with through Christ's awesome strength.

Have you been living your life on your own strength, thinking you can handle it alone? Can you truly say you put your faith and trust in God more than your own abilities? Commit to surrendering every area of your life, including sports, to the strength of God. Let Him be your center and push everything—sports, life, success, challenges, sickness—to the outer rim.

Go

1. What would you do if you found out today that you were terminally ill?
2. Is God at the center of your life? If not, what do you need to change in order to put God at the center?
3. What distractions need to be pushed into the "outer rim"? How can you accomplish this?

Workout

John 11:4; Romans 5:2–5; Isaiah 41:18–20

Overtime

Lord Jesus, thank You for being my hope and strength. Help me push aside anything that is distracting me from focusing on Your love and promises. I don't want to live my life in my own strength; I commit every area of my life to You. You are my center. Amen.

journal

17

Play with Purpose

RUTH RILEY

Ready

> "According to the grace given to us, we have different gifts: If prophecy, use it according to the standard of one's faith; if service, in service; if teaching, in teaching; if exhorting, in exhortation; giving, with generosity; leading, with diligence; showing mercy, with cheerfulness."—Romans 12:6–8

Set

I've been blessed to accomplish some amazing feats that only a handful of female basketball players have achieved. During my career, I've been honored to play on an NCAA National Championship team, a WNBA Championship team, and an Olympic gold-medal team. At Notre Dame, I hit the game-winning shot and was voted the 2001 Final Four's Most Outstanding Player. With the Detroit Shock, I was named the 2003 WNBA Finals MVP. At the 2004 Olympics in Greece, however, I had a completely different experience.

I was the twelfth and final player chosen for the US team. I knew going into the competition that I would not be a significant contributor, but I was nonetheless determined to prepare for whatever I was asked to do. Every day in practice I had the opportunity to guard Lisa Leslie, one of the best players in the world. And that was my role.

In Romans 12:6–8, the apostle Paul teaches us that we all have God-given gifts, and we are called to use those gifts for His purpose. This is true for all competitors, and it's true for all aspects of our lives. As athletes, it might be the difference between leading the team and providing support from the bench. As Christians, it might be the difference between speaking publicly from a platform and serving others anonymously. But no matter what our role or responsibility might be, it's important that we remember to play with purpose, live our lives with humility, and desire to make a difference through the love of Christ.

Go

1. What role do you currently play on your sports team? Are you satisfied with that role? Explain.
2. What do you think it means to "play with purpose"? Are you currently playing with purpose? Why or why not?
3. What can you start doing today that will allow you to embrace that principle? Name three different things you can do.

Workout

1 Corinthians 12:27–31; Colossians 3:23; John 15:16

Overtime

Lord, I want to play with purpose. I want to embrace my role and embrace the gifts and abilities with which You have blessed me. Help me transfer this principle beyond the field of competition and into every aspect of my life. Amen.

journal

journal

18

What's Your Purpose?

BRIAN ROBERTS

Ready

"The LORD will fulfill His purpose for me. LORD, Your love is eternal; do not abandon the work of Your hands."—Psalm 138:8

Set

I've been in the major leagues for over ten years with the Baltimore Orioles. Looking back, I can think of specific guys who were crucial to my development and maturity as a person and a baseball player. Now, as a veteran, I feel it's my role to share what I've learned from my experiences in the same way those guys did with me when I was younger.

Just like David says in Psalm 138, I know the Lord has a purpose for me, and He will fulfill it. I've tried over the years to grow in my understanding of that purpose. As a Christian competitor, I try to use every opportunity I can to share the gospel of Christ along with the struggles I've faced and lessons God has taught me along the way. I have realized that my purpose goes far beyond just playing the game of baseball. God has purposed this sport as my mission field.

We've all been put here by God to be lights for Him, and we've each been given our unique gifts. It is up to us to recognize those gifts and use them for God's glory. We must be willing to use our sport, no matter the level of competition, to fulfill His purposes and to share the amazing gift of His love and grace. It should be our ultimate goal to have those around us—teammates, coaches, fans—see Christ in how we perform within our sport.

And even though we will make mistakes, sometimes secretly and other times in front of the whole world, God's grace is sufficient enough to pick us up and continue to use us for His purposes. His plans are larger than our faults, and He will always fulfill the purpose He has set for us. Never forget, His love and mercies endure forever.

Go

1. What do you feel is your God-given purpose? How does that purpose apply to your athletic or coaching career?
2. Have you ever felt that your inadequacies limit God's purpose for your life? What are some Scriptures that refute that belief?
3. How can you encourage others to pursue and fulfill God's purpose in their lives?

Workout

Psalm 19; Hosea 14:9; 1 Corinthians 3:1–11

Overtime

Almighty Father, You've given us each a specific purpose in this life. Let it be our passion to find that purpose and share Your saving message through it. As competitors and coaches, allow us to never take the position of influence we have for granted. Let it always be an honor to point people to You and Your glory. Amen.

journal

journal

19

Undivided Attention

DONNA NOONAN

Ready

"Teach me Your way, Yahweh, and I will live by Your truth. Give me an undivided mind to fear Your name."—Psalm 86:11

Set

As athletes, we know the importance of mental focus, staying in the present, and not letting distractions draw us away from the play at hand. Whether it is standing over a four-foot putt to win the US Open, shooting a free throw to tie the game, or reading defenses, all skills require training and the ability to give our undivided attention to the task at hand. It's often called "being in the zone."

Our relationship with the Lord requires the same type of training and mind-set. Just like our coaches teach us proper techniques, the Lord teaches us through His Word. He will teach us, but we have to be willing to listen and apply the lessons.

An athlete does not become successful by sitting at practice once a week and listening to the coach. It takes daily learning and practice to improve performance. How well would you play in a game if all you did was listen to a podcast from your coach once a week? Isn't it just as crazy to think that we can have a strong relationship with the Lord simply by attending church on Sunday?

If you are already spending daily time in God's Word, way to go! If not, are you willing to put in the time to learn His way? God desires so much more for us than what we often want for ourselves. To know Him in a deep and personal way can only come from having a mind focused on Him.

Go

1. What does it mean to have an undivided mind? Do you have mental focus when you study God's Word?

2. What does it look like to live according to His way on a daily basis? On your team? At home? At school?

3. What are some things you are willing to change in order to spend more time learning God's Word? Name three different ways you can do this.

Workout

Psalm 86:1–17; Luke 9:23; 1 Timothy 4:8; 2 Timothy 2:4

Overtime

Father, just like I have mental focus when I practice and compete, help me to be undivided in my love for You every day. Help me to make it a priority every day to spend time with You in prayer and in Your Word. Amen.

journal

journal

20

Eyes on the Target

CHARLOTTE SMITH

Ready

"And climbing out of the boat, Peter started walking on water and came toward Jesus. But when
he saw the strength of the wind, he was afraid.
And beginning to sink he cried out, 'Lord save
me!'"—Matthew 14:29–30

Set

One of the oldest acronyms in basketball is BEEF.
The B is for "balance." The first E is for "eyes on
target." The second E is for "elbow straight." And

the F is for "follow through." Each one is important, but plenty of shots go into the basket even if the shooter is off balance, has bent elbows, or doesn't follow through. However, seldom will a ball find the hoop if the shooter's eyes aren't fixed on the target. Each player has his or her own target in their respective sport. A pitcher in baseball must get the ball over the plate. A swimmer needs to reach the other end of the pool. A pole vaulter has to clear the crossbar.

As important as goals are within sports, at the heart of every great Christian competitor should be the discipline of focusing on a greater purpose. Just look at what taking one's eyes off the target produced in the life of the disciple Peter in Matthew 14. He wanted to walk on water with Jesus and did so until he shifted his eyes from Christ to the fierce wind. He became fearful and began to sink.

Likewise, we will start sinking in our lives if we focus on the tumult that surrounds us. We must allow the Holy Spirit to be our guide, reminding us that with Christ, all is well with our souls. No matter the final score, past injury, or pressure to succeed, if we fix our eyes on Christ—our target—and trust His faithful provision, we will be able to accomplish His purposes, both in our game and in our lives.

Go

1. What's your ultimate target? Why did you choose this?
2. When pressure comes, do you stay focused or become distracted? What can help you stay focused on the target?
3. How can you keep yourself from shifting your eyes off God? Name three different ways.

Workout

Luke 2:30; John 10:27; 1 Corinthians 16:13

Overtime

Lord, keep me grounded in my faith. Help me to keep my eyes lifted to the hills from where all my help comes. Help me to always fix my eyes on You so that my faith will never waver. Amen.

journal

journal

21

Finish the Race

SARAH ROBERTS

Ready

"I have fought the good fight, I have finished the
race, I have kept the faith."—2 Timothy 4:7

Set

Less than halfway into the 1968 Mexico City Olympic marathon, Tanzanian runner John Stephen Akhwari's dream of gold was shattered. Unaccustomed
to the city's high altitude, he began cramping early
on in the race but managed to stick close to the

leaders. Then, as runners jockeyed for position near the eleven-mile marker, he collided with another athlete. Akhwari fell hard to the pavement, dislocating his knee and hitting his shoulder and head. Badly bleeding, he picked himself up and continued running.

Akhwari was the last out of the fifty-seven competitors (eighteen dropped out) to finish. And even though there were only a few thousand people left in the stands, he crossed the finish line to a standing ovation. When interviewed the next day as to why he continued to run so badly injured with no chance of winning, he answered, "My country did not send me five thousand miles to start the race; they sent me five thousand miles to finish the race."

John Stephen Akhwari was a competitor because he knew he wasn't in the Olympics to start a race but to finish it. The apostle Paul was also a competitor because he realized that God did not have him on earth merely to start his spiritual race but to fight, to finish, and to keep the faith in the middle of it. Jesus served as our ultimate example of a competitor, knowing His purpose wasn't to just begin His race of redeeming all humankind but to complete it at the cross by saying, "It is finished" (John 19:30). As Christian athletes, we are also called to finish every race we run, whether in our sport or in life. No matter how badly we are beaten down or injured, through Christ's strength we can persevere and cross any finish line set before us.

Go

1. Have you ever been tempted to quit? What was the outcome? Why is it better to finish strong?

2. Like Paul, how can you keep the faith as a competitor?

3. What are some areas in your life in which God's calling you to finish strong? Name three different ways that you can finish strong and keep the faith.

Workout

Philippians 4:13; 2 Corinthians 8:11

Overtime

Lord, help me to finish the races that You have set before me. I look to You for guidance, strength, and courage in all that I do and say. I want to finish strong and keep the faith in my sport and in my life. Amen.

journal

journal

22

Grinders

CHARLES GEE

Ready

"Therefore, my dear brothers, be steadfast, immovable, always excelling in the Lord's work, knowing that your labor in the Lord is not in vain."—1 Corinthians 15:58

Set

Everyone loves "grinders"! A grinder is an athlete who succeeds through hard work and determination rather than exceptional talent or skill. Grinders show up every day, they are eager to work, and they place team before self. They welcome each day as a chance to get better individually and as a team. Grinders believe the words of English writer Samuel Johnson: "Great works are not accomplished by strength, but by perseverance." Hard work over a period of time is usually rewarded.

God knows and comes alongside those who are committed to doing His will. "Grinding for God" is never in vain. We must not allow ourselves to get discouraged or give up. God wants us to keep showing up ready to work and putting the needs of others first. He will take our service and use it for His purpose. He will give us the strength to persevere when times get tough. It's a new day— keep grinding!

Go

1. When others see the way you play and carry yourself, would they call you a "grinder"? Why or why not?

2. Why are some athletes afraid of hard work? Are you afraid of hard work? Why or why not?

3. What does it look like to be a "grinder for God"? How can you commit to doing God's will right now?

Workout

Proverbs 14:23; Luke 5:5; 2 Timothy 4:5

Overtime

Father, thank You for loving me. Teach me and equip me to be a grinder for You. May I never give up, give in, or give out in my service to You. Please use my service to accomplish Your divine plans and purposes for my life. Amen.

journal

journal

23

Run to Win

Sarah Roberts

Ready

"Don't you know that the runners in a stadium all race, but only one receives the prize? Run in such a way to win the prize. Now everyone who competes exercises self-control in everything. However, they do it to receive a crown that will fade away, but we a crown that will never fade away. Therefore I do not run like one who runs aimlessly or box like one beating the air. Instead, I discipline my body and bring it under strict control, so that after preaching to others, I myself will not be disqualified."—1 Corinthians 9:24–27

Set

There are a lot of people in this world who play sports or participate in athletics, but not all of them are competitors. The difference? A competitor plays with purpose. A competitor trains to win. A competitor plays to win. A competitor runs to win. A true competitor doesn't just play to have fun but to achieve the ultimate goal of victory.

Paul understood the heart of a competitive athlete and knew that as Christian athletes we must train our hearts spiritually like we train our bodies physically—with purpose. As followers of Jesus, our purpose in this life is to train our hearts to love like Jesus, to serve others like Jesus, and to put our faith and hope in the Father for every area of our lives, like Jesus did.

Jesus said it this way in John 10:10: "My purpose is to give them a rich and satisfying life" (NLT). When we have Christ in our lives, we are not just living but enjoying true life—life that is rich and satisfying, life that has purpose, and life that is running to win.

Go

1. As an athlete, how do you train your body to win? What is the outcome?

2. As a Christian, how do you train your heart to win? What is the outcome?

3. Write down three spiritual disciplines you can implement each day to train your heart to love more like Christ. How can you start practicing these disciplines right away?

Workout

Romans 12:1–2; Colossians 3:23

Overtime

God, thank You for loving me so much that You were willing to run Your race with purpose, all the way to the cross. Help me to focus my life on the purposes You have set before me as an athlete and follower of You. Amen.

journal

journal

24

Be Courageous

MATT CULLEN

Ready

"Haven't I commanded you: be strong and courageous? Do not be afraid or discouraged, for the LORD your God is with you wherever you go."—Joshua 1:9

Set

As an NHL player, I've never been quick to admit my fears, but I've definitely had them. When facing Edmonton in game seven of the 2006 Stanley Cup

Finals, I was more nervous than I'd ever been in my athletic career. Leaning on God during that game helped me find strength to face my fears head-on. We ended up winning the game and the Stanley Cup, a first for the Carolina Hurricanes.

When our third son, Joey, was born, I dealt with a different kind of fear. I had just been traded to Ottawa, and we were in the playoffs at Pittsburgh. My wife, Bridget, went into labor, and I couldn't get home in time for the delivery. When I got word that Joey was having problems with his lungs, I had to rely heavily on my relationship with the Lord to keep fear from creeping in. He gave me peace to trust that He was taking care of my son and everything would be okay.

Fear is a natural reaction and something we all have to face from time to time. But the Bible clearly tells us that we *don't* have to be afraid when troublesome circumstances come our way. Joshua 1:9 encourages us that to conquer fear, we need to remember that God's always with us, no matter what.

The truth is that we only give in to fear when we fail to fully trust God. So instead of succumbing to our fears, let's courageously acknowledge them and then take them to God in prayer. He will faithfully give us the courage to walk through any challenge we face within our sport, our health, our finances, our relationships, and every other aspect of our lives.

Go

1. When have you experienced fear? How did you handle it?
2. How is fear related to a lack of trust in God? Why is it important to fully trust God with every detail of your life?
3. Read Joshua 1:9. What are some of God's characteristics that make it easier to overcome fear? What can you do on a daily basis to trust God more?

Workout

Isaiah 41:10; Psalm 23; Philippians 4:6

Overtime

Lord, give me courage when life's troubles come my way. Remind me of who You are so that I can be courageous and capable of facing any trying situation. Help me to fully trust You in every aspect of my life. Amen.

journal

journal

25

Single-Handed

CHARLES GEE

Ready

"For as the body is one and has many parts, and all the parts of that body, though many, are one body—so also is Christ."—1 Corinthians 12:12

Set

Have you ever been guilty of trying to coach "single-handedly"? If you have, you know from experience that it's not the most efficient or effective way to get things done. As a young head coach, I had the attitude that if it was going to get done the way I wanted, I had to do it myself.

Looking back, it's not too hard for me to see a little pride and ego in my methods. I wanted to prove that I was capable of getting the job done. Little did I realize that not only was I wearing myself out, I was also denying my coaching staff the opportunity to grow and develop their own coaching skills. As I matured, I began to understand that trying to do things by myself would always limit the scope of what could be done and make me old at an early age.

The apostle Paul reminds us that we need each other. Yes, we can accomplish great things with the gifts God has given us, but we can do so much more if we connect our gifts with the gifts of others. When the people of God come together as a team, watch out! There is something about a common goal that naturally connects people. This is true in athletics, business, church, and ministry. We might call it having "good chemistry." What actually happens is that we stop thinking about ourselves and start thinking about how we can get the job done. We stop trying to do it all and simply begin to do our part. God intended us to be unified. Regardless of where God has placed us, He has others ready to join the team as we pursue our common goal. Don't make the mistake of trying to run the race on your own.

Go

1. When have you been guilty of trying to accomplish an athletic goal single-handedly? What was the outcome?

2. What unique gifts has God given you? Are you using these gifts to glorify God and connect with the gifts of others on your team?

3. What is the best team you have been a part of? Why? What were the unique gifts that each person brought to the team?

Workout

John 17:20–23; Philippians 2:1–3

Overtime

Lord, forgive me for trying to do it all by myself. Teach me to trust the teammates You put beside me each day. Help me to use the unique gifts You have given me to make our team stronger and better to accomplish Your plans and purposes. In Jesus's name. Amen.

journal

journal

26

Answering the Call

A D R I E N N E S H E R W O O D

Ready

"For we are His creation, created in Christ Jesus for good works, which God prepared ahead of time so that we should walk in them."—Ephesians 2:10

Set

When I was thirteen, I found my first love: basketball. One day when I was in seventh grade, a repairman came to work on my parents' house while I was shooting hoops. I don't remember his name or what he looked like, but he made a comment that stuck with me.

"What's your name, miss?" he asked. I mumbled a response between baskets and then asked him why. "I'll remember it when you're playing in the WNBA."

It was a magical moment. That comment lit a fire in me, and I worked even harder than before. The idea of playing in the WNBA was the most amazing thing I thought could ever happen in my life.

A few years later, though, God showed me something even more amazing. He used my love for basketball to draw me into a personal relationship with Jesus, and then He called me to share my faith with hundreds of athletes and coaches through the platform of FCA.

Honestly, I wasn't initially interested in this plan. I wanted to be a professional athlete! My heart was broken when I didn't achieve the goal the repairman and I had set that day. But now that I'm more than ten years beyond that day, I'm so grateful that the Lord allowed me to answer His call for me and not my own. I can look back and see His handiwork in ways I'd never have seen without His intervention.

Go

1. Do you trust God with your future? Why or why not?
2. Have you answered His call to a relationship with Christ? If not, what is holding you back from making that decision?
3. Are you holding on tighter to your dreams than to Jesus? What happens when you let go of your dreams and hold on to Jesus's plans for you?

Workout

Psalms 119:105; 127:1; Isaiah 55:8–9; 1 Corinthians 3:7

Overtime

Father, what is Your will for my life? Please make it clear as I continue to seek You. I want to let go of my dreams and grab on to the incredible plan You have for my life. Help me to fully trust in You and not myself. In Jesus's name I pray. Amen.

journal

27

Remain in Me

FLECEIA COMEAUX

Ready

"I am the vine; you are the branches. The one who remains in Me and I in him produces much fruit, because you can do nothing without Me. . . . If you remain in Me and My words remain in you, ask whatever you want and it will be done for you. My Father is glorified by this: that you produce much fruit and prove to be My disciples."—John 15:5, 7–8

Set

In John 15, Jesus is giving a final charge to His disciples about staying connected to the true vine. He encourages, reiterates, and implores them to stay connected to Him. I often find it unbelievably significant when Christ repeats Himself. There is a fundamental principle that He is trying to relay to the people of God and specifically His disciples.

As the text unfolds, three promises are identified as consequences of remaining in Him: we will produce much fruit, we can ask whatever we want and it will be done, and we will glorify the Father.

What athlete or coach doesn't want to produce fruit? You don't work out or practice not to produce—you do it with a goal in mind. Who doesn't want their prayers answered? When you pray over your season or your team, do you sincerely want God to answer? Yes!

And which one of us does not have a desire to glorify the Father during our performance? Your effort, work, and striving in sports and life must end in His glory. When we do not remain in Him, we are setting ourselves up for failure. I don't know about you, but I choose to stay connected to the true vine and receive all the benefits that follow.

"To remain" means to continue in the same state. You have too much at stake as an athlete and believer to be detached from the Father at any time or in any way. Remain in Him, and let His Word remain in you.

Go

1. Are you remaining in Him throughout your season? Why or why not?
2. Is His Word remaining in you as you coach, teach, or perform? If not, what can you do to hide His Word in your heart?
3. What type of fruit are you producing? Are you producing fruit that will last, or are you just competing and coaching for the temporary rewards?

Workout

1 John 2:5–6; Psalm 119:9–11

Overtime

Father, it is Your desire that I remain in You and Your Word remain in me. Please help me to stay close to the things that bring me true wisdom, power, and peace. Let my actions reflect Your principles, and let my decisions reflect Your heart. In Jesus's name. Amen.

journal

journal

28

Breaking Free

Lauren Holiday

Ready

> "Now the Lord is the Spirit, and where the Spirit
> of the Lord is, there is freedom."—2 Corinthians
> 3:17

Set

In 2008, I made my first US Olympic Soccer Team.
I was still in college and one of the youngest players
on the roster. I was also replacing star player Abby
Wambach, who couldn't compete due to an injury.

Then in 2012, I was chosen for the Olympic squad again, but this time I was considered a veteran with several major matches under my belt, including the 2008 Olympic gold-medal game and the 2010 FIFA World Cup. While the two situations were very different, they were also very much the same. There was a great deal of pressure that came with the job.

The pressure of high expectations can be difficult to manage. If you have a bad game, you can't blame anyone but yourself. If you have a great game, you can be tempted to get prideful and unknowingly set yourself up to fall. The hardest part is playing free and not allowing the pressure to negatively impact your performance and steal your joy in the process.

In order to break free of the pressure that comes with expectations, there are some important steps that you must take. First of all, make sure that your confidence is in Christ—not in yourself. Secondly, understand that your identity is in Him. And finally, always keep in mind that your sport should be, as it says in Romans 12:1, your spiritual act of worship. Whatever talent Christ has blessed you with ultimately belongs to Him.

Those steps will help relieve the pressure from high expectations. They will also bring you true joy and allow you to give God the glory in everything you do.

Go

1. Describe a time when you felt pressure as an athlete. How did it impact your performance?
2. Of the three steps listed, which ones have you applied to your life? Which ones are difficult to walk out?
3. Read 2 Corinthians 3:17. How might inviting His Spirit into your athletic life bring freedom and help you better deal with pressure?

Workout

Romans 12:1–2; 2 Timothy 1:7; John 8:32

Overtime

Lord, I want to break free from worldly expectations and the pressures that accompany them. Transform my way of thinking and fill my heart with the kind of joy that only You can bring. Amen.

journal

journal

29

Fired Up

Jimmy Page

Ready

"Consider it a great joy, my brothers, whenever you experience various trials, knowing that the testing of your faith produces endurance. But endurance must do its complete work, so that you may be mature and complete, lacking nothing."
—James 1:2–4

Set

Cut from the team. Lost the state title. Playing time disappeared. Your mistake cost the team a win. As a competitor, all these things are considered tough trials. Add to that academic pressure or conflict at home, and you can feel overwhelmed.

In Daniel 3, we read the account of how Shadrach, Meshach, and Abednego faced one of the hottest trials in history. When they refused to bow down and worship a false god, they were literally thrown into the fiery furnace.

Adversity always brings opportunity. When those men took their stand and fell into the fire, the soldiers who threw them in were killed instantly, but Shadrach, Meshach, and Abednego were unharmed. When the king saw the unwavering faith and courage of these men and then witnessed this great miracle, he immediately recognized that "there is no other god who is able to deliver like this" (v. 29). When others see how we persevere and trust through trials, they believe.

Character is uncovered in crisis and formed in the fire. It will be *revealed and refined*. God forms our character the same way He forms diamonds—with time, pressure, and heat. When the element carbon is forced to go deeper beneath the surface of the earth, it encounters extreme temperatures and pressure. Those extreme conditions make diamonds. And when they rise again to the surface, they display the brilliance of the light.

God uses trials to make *us* unshakable and *Him* unmistakable. The more heat and pressure we feel, the more heart and presence of God we experience. When we face trials, we can do it with joy, knowing God uses pressure and pain to produce perseverance and maturity, which can be witnessed by others. Let your character be formed in the fire and see how lives are transformed.—*Adapted from WisdomWalks Sports*

Go

1. Have you experienced adversity that's tested your faith? How did you respond to the situation?
2. How did that adversity lead to opportunity? How did you take the opportunity?
3. What's the purpose of suffering in this life? Do you experience God in suffering?

Workout

1 Peter 4:12–16; 2 Corinthians 1:3–6; Proverbs 17:17

Overtime

Father, I know that storms are not optional but inevitable. Let me rejoice when I face the "fire," knowing You are refining me in the process. Use the storms in my life to make me unshakable and You unmistakable. Amen.

journal

journal

30

Under Authority

SARAH RENNICKE

Ready

"Everyone must submit to the governing authorities, for there is no authority except from God, and those that exist are instituted by God."—Romans 13:1

Set

When a coach and player don't see eye to eye, it can be an overwhelmingly frustrating experience for everyone on the team. Heads collide, visions blur, and there's a lack of motivation to perform. It's a fatal combination for any team.

As athletes, we all want our coaches to be sources of inspiration and solid teaching. At times, though, we wind up on teams where that's not the case. Every practice is daunting, and the mental energy it takes to focus drains our physical energy and performance.

When we're under an authority figure who may be overbearing, negative, and not leading in God's direction, our instinct tells us to disregard their place over us, become discouraged, and wish away our season. But it's the season of life we've been given, and we can't waste time grumbling and wanting to take the easy way out.

In Scripture God clearly tells us to persevere, to fix our eyes on Jesus, and to trust that He will make something good from the situation. The people He has put above us are by His institution, and though it may be difficult to unclench the fists around our hearts, we must open ourselves to hearing from God in new ways through our obedience.

And we *will* hear and grow. Because God often uses what we fight most to disclose more of Himself to us through the process.

Go

1. What areas of your life do you have a hard time letting someone else control? Why is it hard for you to give up control?
2. How can you enter a state of submission to those you don't agree with?
3. How will you benefit from obeying God and His commands?

Workout

Luke 12:4–5; Hebrews 12:9; James 4:6–8

Overtime

Lord, please help me submit to those who are over me, even when it's difficult to follow their leadership. Give me the grace to serve them, and let me be a light to show them You. In Jesus's name I pray. Amen.

journal

journal

31

The Thankful Competitor

DAN BRITTON

Ready

"And whatever you do, in word or in deed, do everything in the name of the Lord Jesus, giving thanks to God the Father through Him."
—Colossians 3:17

Set

A Christian competitor is a thankful competitor. Every time you step onto the field of competition, your heart is exploding with thankfulness, because you are abundantly grateful for God's blessings. You have a deep conviction that your athletic abilities have come from Him alone. Every stride, swing, shot, pass, goal, and point is a response to God's goodness. The way you compete is marked with a "thank you, God" because you count all of His blessings in your life.

You have been given much by the Lord, and you are simply grateful for the opportunity to compete. Your sweat is an offering of thanks to Him. There is no room for pride in a heart full of thankfulness. A thankful competitor is a humble competitor.

When you are thankful, you don't try to impress others. You don't care if you are starting when you are overwhelmed with gratitude to be part of a team. You don't put unrealistic expectations on your teammates' shoulders when you realize God's grace in your life. You don't care about the scoreboard when your definition of winning is becoming more like Jesus every time you compete.

You don't view competition as crushing your opponent when you desire to play in such a way that elevates all participants to a higher level of competition. You are not consumed with what others think when you are focused on an audience of One.

You don't criticize teammates when you believe the best about them. You don't have to play for others when you already feel God's pleasure. Be a thankful competitor! With a grateful heart, much can be accomplished. Let the power of thanksgiving change the way you compete. A Christian competitor is a thankful competitor.

Go

1. What are you most grateful for? How do you show your gratitude?
2. How can you become a more thankful competitor? Name three different ways.
3. When do you struggle to give thanks? When is it easy?

Workout

2 Corinthians 9:10–11; 1 Timothy 1:12; Colossians 3:15; 1 Corinthians 15:57

Overtime

Father, I want to be a thankful competitor. Whatever I do or say, I will do it all in the name of the Lord Jesus, giving thanks to You. Use the power of an attitude of gratitude to change the way I compete and help me to focus on an audience of One. Amen.

journal

journal

Contributors

Dan Britton is a husband, father, author, speaker, coach, marathoner, and former professional lacrosse player. He has coauthored four books and also authored and edited twelve additional FCA books. He serves as FCA's international executive vice president and lives in Overland Park, Kansas.

Tamika Catchings is a WNBA forward for the Indiana Fever. She is a four-time WNBA Defensive Player of the Year, the league's 2011 MVP, and a two-time Olympic gold medalist. She is also founder of the Catch the Stars Foundation, a mentoring program for young people in Indianapolis.

Fleceia Comeaux serves as the area director for the South Houston FCA office. She is a graduate of the University of Houston, where she played basketball and soccer.

Matt Cullen is a professional ice hockey center-man. Cullen is currently a member of the Pittsburgh Penguins and resides in West Fargo, North Dakota, with his wife and three children.

Blake Elder is an FCA volunteer in North Carolina.

Mike Fisher is a center and an alternate captain for the Nashville Predators. He has made eleven play-off appearances in sixteen NHL seasons and was a member of the 2007 Eastern Conference championship team in Ottawa. In 2012, Fisher received the prestigious NHL Foundation Player Award.

Charles Gee has been teaching and coaching for over forty years. He serves FCA in Coaches Ministry, is chaplain for the South Carolina Athletic Coaches Association, and lives in Lexington, South Carolina.

Jayson Gee is the head men's basketball coach at Longwood University. He has over twenty-six years of coaching experience and has coached in two NCAA Division I tournaments and four NCAA Division II tournaments. In 2015, Coach Gee was presented the 2015 FCA John Lotz Barnabas Award.

Tobin Heath is a midfielder for the US Women's National Soccer Team. She won Olympic gold medals at the 2008 Beijing Games and the 2012 London Games, and was a starter on the 2015 FIFA Women's World Cup gold-medal team. Previously, Heath won three NCAA championships at the University of North Carolina.

Hal Hiatt is a multi-area director for FCA in coastal North and South Carolina. He is also the pastor of First Baptist Church in Carolina Beach, North Carolina, where he and his wife, Sherrie, make their home. Hal and Sherrie have been together in ministry for thirty-two years.

Lauren Holiday is a retired professional soccer midfielder and forward. She played for FC Kansas City in the NWSL and the US Women's National Soccer Team. Holiday is a two-time Olympic gold medalist, winning gold with the national team at the 2008 Beijing Summer Olympics and the 2012 London Summer Olympics.

Clint Hurdle is the manager of the Pittsburgh Pirates and former major league outfielder. Previous to his stint with the Pirates, he managed the Colorado Rockies to its first World Series appearance in 2007. Hurdle was named National League Manager of the Year in 2013.

Roger Lipe is the midwest region international co-ordinator for the Fellowship of Christian Athletes, the campus director for Saluki FCA at Southern Illinois University in Carbondale, and serves the midwest region in developing sports chaplaincy ministries.

Joe Matera was called into full-time ministry at the age of forty and pioneered surf ministry with FCA, serving as the national director of board sports. He believed in living a life with God in the center, walking forward in faith, passion, and humor. He went home to be with the Lord in 2013.

Sean McNamara's spiritual journey began in 1992 when he accepted Christ as a young lacrosse player while attending an FCA camp. After graduating from Randolph-Macon College in 1999—where he played NCAA Division III lacrosse and served as team captain and FCA campus leader—he joined FCA staff as the national director of FCA lacrosse and the first full-time staff person to oversee that ministry. He has served as vice president of field ministry of the northeast region and Canada since 2010 and is excited to see God continue to build great things within the northeast region.

Elana Meyers-Taylor is a member of the US Women's Bobsled Team. She has won two Olympic medals, including a silver medal at the 2014 Sochi Games and a bronze medal at the 2010 Vancouver Games. At the World Championships, Meyers-Taylor has won three gold medals, two silver medals, and two bronze medals.

Donna Noonan is the FCA national director of women's staff development and events. Prior to coming to FCA she directed national championships for the NCAA, including the Women's Final Four. She played collegiate golf and basketball at the University of Georgia as well as coached golf at the NCAA Division I level.

Kerry O'Neill serves on FCA staff in Virginia. He is passionate about developing three-dimensional coaches who will connect with their athletes to reach their full potential.

Jimmy Page serves as a vice president of field ministry for the mid-Atlantic region. He is the author of several bestselling books and resides in Maryland with his wife, Ivelisse, and four children.

Sarah Rennicke is the content writer for Fellowship of Christian Athletes. She loves people and words, and loves weaving them together. She believes that God created creativity to see His handiwork, and that we are all desiring to be seen, known, and loved.

Ruth Riley is a retired professional basketball player, playing most recently for the Atlanta Dream in the WNBA. Riley was the Most Valuable Player in the 2001 and 2003 championship series. She has also played on teams that won the gold medal at the Olympic Games. In 2016 she was named general manager of the San Antonio Stars.

Brian Roberts is a retired professional baseball player. The second baseman made his MLB debut with the Baltimore Orioles in 2001. His final season was for the New York Yankees in 2014.

Sarah Roberts began working for FCA in 2003 as the Oklahoma director of women's ministry, serving female coaches, female athletes, and coaches' wives. She has been married to coach Chris Roberts since 1998 and they have four children.

Adrienne Sherwood serves as the urban soccer director for the Fellowship of Christian Athletes in Atlanta, Georgia. She has been on staff since 2010. She and her husband, Chris, live in the neighborhood famous for Dr. King's birth home and church, the Old Fourth Ward of Atlanta.

Charlotte Smith is a former All-American and two-time All-ACC player and won an ESPN ESPY for Best Female College Basketball Player in 1995. She played professionally for ten years and was an assistant coach at North Carolina for nine seasons before taking the head women's basketball coaching position in 2011 at Elon University.

Rex Stump is the multi-area director for FCA in the northwest Ohio region. Rex focuses on FCA, speaking opportunities, pastoring, and coaching youth sports (including FCA baseball teams). He and his wife, Jenny, have three boys.

Adam Wainwright is a professional baseball starting pitcher for the St. Louis Cardinals. He has won more than 100 games, three All-Star selections, and two Rawlings Gold Glove Awards, and has finished in the top three in the Cy Young Award balloting four times. He married his high school sweetheart, Jenny Curry, and they reside in St. Simon, Georgia, with their three daughters.

Impacting the World for Christ through Sports

The Fellowship of Christian Athletes is touching millions of lives—one heart at a time. Since 1954, the Fellowship of Christian Athletes has been challenging coaches and athletes on the professional, college, high school, junior high, and youth levels to use the powerful medium of athletics to impact the world for Jesus Christ. FCA focuses on serving local communities by equipping, empowering, and encouraging people to make a difference for Christ.

FCA Vision

To see the world impacted for Jesus Christ through the influence of coaches and athletes.

FCA Mission

To present to coaches and athletes, and all whom they influence, the challenge and adventure of receiving Jesus Christ as Savior and Lord, serving Him in their relationships and in the fellowship of the church.

FCA Values

Our relationships will demonstrate steadfast commitment to Jesus Christ and His Word through Integrity, Serving, Teamwork, and Excellence.

Integrity We will demonstrate Christlike wholeness, privately and publicly. (Prov. 11:3)

Serving We will model Jesus's example of serving. (John 13:1–17)

Teamwork We will express our unity in Christ in all our relationships. (Phil. 2:1–4)

Excellence We will honor and glorify God in all we do. (Col. 3:23–24)

Ministries of FCA

The FCA ministries encourage, equip, and empower coaches and athletes on all levels to use the powerful medium of sports to impact their world for Jesus Christ. The FCA ministries, called the 4 C's, are Coaches Ministry, Campus Ministry, Camp Ministry, and Community Ministry.

Coaches: FCA Coaches Ministry is the ministry method to coaches through huddles, events, training, and resources. FCA Coaches Ministry focuses on ministering to the heart of the coach first, and then supporting the coach as they engage with the Four Cs of Ministry.

Campus: The school campus is one of the most strategic mission fields, with over 98 percent of all youth passing through this portal. FCA focuses on equipping, enabling, empowering, and encouraging student athletes, coaches, and adult leaders to impact and influence their campus for Christ.

Camps: Camp is a time of "inspiration and perspiration" for coaches and athletes to reach their potential by offering comprehensive athletic, spiritual, and leadership training. In FCA we offer seven types of camps: Sports Camps, Leadership Camps, Coaches Camps, Power Camps,

Partnership Camps, Team Camps, and International Camps.

Community: FCA Community Ministry is the off-campus opportunities to reach coaches and athletes for Christ through the club and recreation sport environment.

Competitor's Creed

I am a Christian first and last.
I am created in the likeness of God Al-
    mighty to bring Him glory.
I am a member of Team Jesus Christ.
I wear the colors of the Cross.
I am a Competitor now and forever.
I am made to strive, to strain, to stretch, and
    to succeed in the arena of competition.
I am a Christian Competitor and as such,
I face my challenger with the face of Christ.
I do not trust in myself.
I do not boast in my abilities or believe in
    my own strength.
I rely solely on the power of God.
I compete for the pleasure of my Heavenly
    Father, the honor of Christ, and the
    reputation of the Holy Spirit.

My attitude on and off the field is above
reproach—my conduct beyond criticism.
Whether I am preparing, practicing, or
playing, I submit to God's authority and
those He has put over me.
I respect my coaches, officials, teammates,
and competitors out of respect for the
Lord.
My body is the temple of Jesus Christ.
I protect it from within and without.
Nothing enters my body that does not
honor the Living God.
My sweat is an offering to my Master.
My soreness is a sacrifice to my Savior.
I give my all—all the time.
I do not give up. I do not give in. I do not
give out.
I am the Lord's warrior—a competi-
tor by conviction and a disciple of
determination.
I am confident beyond reason because my
confidence lies in Christ.
The results of my effort must result in His
glory.
Let the competition begin.
Let the glory be God's.

Sign the Creed: Go to www.fca.org

© 2017 FCA

Coach's Creed

Pray as though nothing of eternal value
is going to happen in my athletes'
lives unless God does it.

Prepare each practice and game as giving "my utmost for His highest."

Seek not to be served by my athletes for
personal gain, but seek to serve them
as Christ served the church.

Be satisfied not with producing a good
record, but with producing good
athletes.

Attend carefully to my private and pub-
lic walk with God, knowing that the
athlete will never rise to a standard
higher than that being lived by the
coach.

Exalt Christ in my coaching, trusting
   the Lord will then draw athletes to
   Himself.

Desire to have a growing hunger for
   God's Word, for personal obedience,
   for fruit of the spirit, and for salti-
   ness in competition.

Depend solely upon God for
   transformation—one athlete at a
   time.

Preach Christ's word in a Christ-like
   demeanor, on and off the field of
   competition.

Recognize that it is impossible to bring
   glory to both myself and Christ at
   the same time.

Allow my coaching to exude the fruit
   of the Spirit, thus producing Christ-
   like athletes.

Trust God to produce in my athletes
   His chosen purposes, regardless of
   whether the wins are readily visible.

Coach with humble gratitude, as one
   privileged to be God's coach.

© 2017 FCA-Heart of a Coach®

Revised from "The Preacher's Mandate"

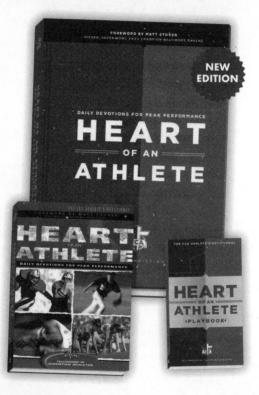